Safari Sam's Wild Animals

Jungle Animals

W

FRANKLIN WATTS

LONDON•SYDNEY

Franklin Watts
First published in Great Britain in 2015 by The Watts Publishing Group

Designed and illustrated by David West

Dewey number 591.734
HB ISBN 978 1 4451 4499 3

Printed in Malaysia

Franklin Watts
An imprint of
Hachette Children's Group
Part of The Watts Publishing Group
Carmelite House
50 Victoria Embankment
London EC4Y 0DZ

An Hachette UK Company
www.hachette.co.uk

www.franklinwatts.co.uk

SAFARI SAM'S WILD ANIMALS JUNGLE ANIMALS
was produced for Franklin Watts by
David West Children's Books, 6 Princeton Court, 55 Felsham Road, London SW15 1AZ

Safari Sam says:
I will tell you something
more about the animal.

Learn what this
animal eats.

Where in the
world is the
animal found?

Its size is revealed!

What animal group
is it – mammal, bird,
reptile, amphibian,
insect, or something
else?

Interesting facts.

Contents

Black Panthers

Black panthers are one of the top **predators** in the jungle. Their dark fur is ideal **camouflage** in the forest's shadows as they stalk their **prey**. Black leopards are found in Africa and Asia. Black jaguars live in South America.

Safari Sam says:
Lions, tigers, leopards and jaguars are all known as panthers. When leopards and jaguars have an unusual black skin and fur colouring, they are called black panthers.

4

Black leopard

Black panthers eat meat and their prey varies from birds and fish to mammals and reptiles.

Black panthers are found in the jungles of Asia, Africa, and South America.

Leopards have a body length of around 1.8 metres.

Panthers are mammals. Mammals have fur and give birth to live young.

A male black jaguar mated with a lioness, who gave birth to a black jaglion.

5

Safari Sam says:
Female boa constrictors give birth to as many as 60 live babies. They start life at 60 centimetres long and grow continually throughout their 25–30 year lives.

Boa constrictors will eat anything they can catch, including birds, deer, monkeys, and wild pigs.

Boa constrictor

Boa Constrictors

The boa constrictor is a large snake that captures its prey with its jaws. It quickly wraps its body around its victim and squeezes it until it **suffocates**. Its jaws stretch wide to swallow large prey whole. After this the snake might not eat for several months.

Boa constrictors are found in Central and South America.

Boa constrictors can grow up to 4 metres long and weigh more than 45 kilogrammes.

Boa constrictors are reptiles and members of the snake family.

The longest boa constrictor ever measured was 5.5 metres long.

Chameleons

These strange-looking lizards come in a variety of sizes and colours. Their eyes can move and focus separately, to observe two different objects at the same time. They capture prey by firing out their long, sticky-tipped tongues.

8

Panther chameleon

Chameleons are mainly insectivores, which means they eat only insects, but some will also eat snails, worms, lizards, amphibians and plant material.

Chameleons inhabit tropical and mountain rainforests, grasslands and sometimes deserts in Africa, Madagascar, the Middle East, southern Europe and southern Asia. They have also been introduced to Hawaii, California and Florida.

Panther chameleons can grow up to 51 centimetres in length.

Chameleons are reptiles are members of the lizard family.

Some chameleons are able to change their skin colour. They do this to signal to each other as well as to blend in with their surroundings.

9

Chimpanzees

Chimpanzees spend much of their time in the trees. They can travel quickly through the leafy canopy of a jungle by swinging from branch to branch. At night they sleep in nests in the tree tops made from branches and leaves.

Chimpanzees are mostly fruit and plant eaters, but they also feed on insects, eggs and meat.

Chimpanzees live in African jungles, woodlands and grasslands.

Chimpanzees grow up to 1.7 metres in height and can weigh up to 59 kilogrammes.

Chimpanzees are mammals and members of the primate family, which also includes humans.

Although they normally walk on all fours, known as knuckle-walking, chimpanzees can also stand and walk upright.

Chimpanzee

11

Safari Sam says:
Like chimpanzees, gorillas use tools for various tasks. One gorilla has been seen testing the depth of a swamp with a stick before wading through it.

Gorilla

Gorillas

Gorillas live in groups called troops. The troop is led by a large male called a silverback, named because of the silver hair that grows on his back at 12 years or over. The troop divide the day between eating, resting and moving to feeding grounds.

Gorillas usually eat fruit, plant shoots and leaves, and occasionally ants and termites.

Gorillas live in jungles in Africa.

Wild male gorillas grow to 1.8 metres tall and weigh up to 180 kilogrammes.

Gorillas are mammals and members of the primate family.

The silverback gorilla protects the members of the troop from predators, such as leopards.

African forest elephant

Safari Sam says:
African forest elephants talk to each other using low calls that can be heard by other elephants several kilometres away. These sounds are too low to be heard by people.

African forest elephants feed on grass, leaves, bark, fruit and other vegetation.

14

Jungle Elephants

These giants of the African jungle have no natural predators. They use their trunk to touch and hold things, and to suck up water for drinking and spraying on their bodies.

African forest elephants are found in the lowland jungles of west and central Africa.

African forest elephants grow to 4 metres in length and weigh around 2.7 metric tons.

Elephants are mammals.

African forest elephants can drink up to 230 litres of water in one day.

Orangutans

Along with gorillas and chimpanzees, orangutans are members of the great ape family. They spend most of their time alone, feeding on fruit in the trees. Young orangutans stay with their mothers for two years before they can start to get about alone. From the age of two, they may travel holding hands with an older orangutan.

Safari Sam says:
The name 'orangutan' comes from the Malay and Indonesian words orang meaning 'person' and hutan meaning 'forest'. So orangutan means 'person of the forest'.

16

Baby orangutan

Orangutans eat mainly fruit but will also eat vegetation, bark, honey, insects and even birds' eggs.

Orangutans are found only in the rainforests of Borneo and Sumatra.

Adult male orangutans can reach 1.85 metres in height and weigh over 120 kilogrammes.

Orangutans are mammals and members of the primate family.

Orangutans make several different types of calls and have even been known to **blow a raspberry**!

17

Safari Sam says:
Parrots, along with the crow family of birds, are among the most intelligent birds. Some **species** can imitate human voices.

Red-and-green macaw

Parrots

Parrots vary in size from small budgerigars to large macaws. Many parrots use their feet like hands to hold nuts while they crack them open with their hooked beaks. Most parrots nest in hollows in trees or in cavities dug into cliffs, banks or the ground.

Most parrots eat seeds, nuts, fruit, buds and other plant material.

Parrots are found in Central and South America, Africa, South Asia and Australasia.

The wingspan of the red-and-green macaw can be up to 125 centimetres, with a total body length of 94 centimetres.

Parrots are birds, which are feathered, two-legged, lay eggs and have wings.

Macaws and some other parrots often eat clay from river banks. The clay is rich in **sodium** which the parrots need to keep healthy.

Poison dart frogs

These brightly-coloured frogs are highly poisonous. They are often called 'dart frogs', because local tribespeople use the frogs' poison on the tips of their blowdarts. They then fire the darts through long blowpipes at prey, such as monkeys.

Poison dart frogs feed on all types of insects.

Poison dart frogs can be found in the jungles of Central and South America.

Most poison dart frogs are very small – less than 1.5 centimetres in length – although a few grow to 6 centimetres long.

Poison dart frogs are amphibians, which means they can live in and out of water.

Adult frogs lay their eggs in moist places. Once the eggs hatch, the adult piggybacks the tadpoles, one at a time, to a pool of water.

Safari Sam says:
Poison dart frogs are brightly coloured to ward off predators. Even non-poisonous species scare off predators with their bold colours!

Poison dart frog

Tigers

Tigers live a solitary life. They are excellent hunters, using their striped coat to camouflage themselves and ambush their prey from the jungle shadows. They are strong swimmers and are often found cooling off in ponds, lakes and rivers.

Tigers mostly feed on large and medium-sized animals from water buffalo to small deer and wild boar.

Tigers are an **endangered** species and can be found only in Eastern and Southeast Asia.

Tigers can reach 3.4 metres and weigh over 300 kilogrammes.

Tigers are mammals and members of the cat family.

A tiger can go up to two weeks without eating, but then can eat up to 34 kilogrammes of meat in one meal.

Tiger

Safari Sam says:
Tigers can be different colours. Both white tigers and golden tigers have been reported in the wild.

23

Glossary

blow a raspberry
To stick out your tongue and blow to make a rasping sound.

camouflage
To blend in with the natural surroundings.

endangered
When a species' survival is under threat because its numbers are decreasing.

predator
An animal that hunts other animals for food.

prey
An animal that is hunted by another for food.

sodium
An essential mineral for many animals' diets.

species
A group of animals that have similar characteristics and can produce offspring.

suffocate
To die from lack of air.

Index